THE AMERICAN POETRY SERIES

Giraffe
How the Plains Indians Got Horses
In the Outer Dark

OUT-OF-THE-BODY TRAVEL

STANLEY PLUMLY

OUT-OF-THE-BODY TRAVEL

THE ECCO PRESS
NEW YORK

DESIGNED BY EARL TIDWELL

Copyright © by Stanley Plumly, 1974, 1975, 1976
All rights reserved
First published by The Ecco Press in 1977
1 West 30th Street, New York, N.Y. 10001

Published simultaneously in Canada by
The Macmillan Company of Canada Limited

Printed in the United States of America
The Ecco Press logo by Ahmed Yacoubi

Library of Congress Cataloging in Publication Data
Plumly, Stanley, 1939–
    Out-of-the-Body Travel
    (The American poetry series; v. 10)
    I. Title.
PS3566.L7809   811'.5'4   76-46174
ISBN 0-912-94635-0

Grateful acknowledgment is made to the following publications in which
these poems first appeared: *Antaeus*: "Anothering," "Cows," "December,
1945," "For Hope," "Linoleum: Breaking Down," "Small Dark Streets."
Bobbs-Merrill (in *American Poets in 1976*): "Horse in the Cage." *Field*:
"For Esther," "Peppergrass." *The Humanist*: "Six Poems . . ." (here
titled "Two Poems"), "Wrong Side of the River." *Iowa Review*: "The
Tree." *The Nation*: "After Grief," "Such Counsels," "Say Summer."
The New Review: "Brothers & Sisters." *The New Yorker*: "Rainbow,"
"The Iron Lung." *The Ohio Review*: "Early Meadow-Rue," "Ghazal/
Insomnia," "Out-of-the-Body Travel," "This Poem," "Wages."
Salmagundi: "Why I Lie Down in You" (here titled "Sonnet").

The epigraph has at least two sources—Captain John Smith and Søren
Kierkegaard.

I would like to thank the John Simon Guggenheim Foundation for a grant
which made completion of this book possible.   —S.P.

for Esther

CONTENTS

I

II

he who will not work shall not eat
and only he who was troubled shall find rest

he who will not work shall not eat
and only he who was troubled shall find rest

I

COWS

Sometimes when you couldn't sleep it off
you'd go outside and sing to the cows.
And they'd sing back, *moon, moon.*
I could hear you all night from my room,
a bull in stall, blowing across
the top of the bottle. I can hear you now,
here, in this room, as I have, poem
after poem. As just a moment ago, almost
dawn, you came breaking back into the house.
My father's house, my room. You couldn't
sleep it off. You went out into the dark,
got lost, almost. I hear the cows.
And the moon's still up, the doomed moon.
And all this time I've stayed awake with you.

THE IRON LUNG

So this is the dust that passes through porcelain,
so this is the unwashed glass left over from supper,
so this is the air in the attic, in August,
and this the down on the breath of the sleeper . . .

If we could fold our arms, but we can't.
If we could cross our legs, but we can't.
If we could put the mind to rest . . .
But our fathers have set this task before us.

My face moons in the mirror, weightless,
without air, my head propped like a penny.
I'm dressed in a shoe, ready to walk out
of here. I'm wearing my father's body.

I remember my mother standing in the doorway
trying to tell me something. The day is thick
with the heat rising from the road. I am
too far away. She looks like my sister.

And I am dreaming of my mother in a doorway
telling my father to die or go away.
It is the front door, and my drunken father falls
to the porch on his knees like one of his children.

It is precisely at this moment I realize
I have polio and will never walk again.
And I am in the road on my knees, like my father,
but as if I were growing into the ground

I can neither move nor rise.
The neighborhood is gathering, and now
my father is lifting me into the ambulance
among the faces of my family. His face is

a blur or a bruise and he holds me
as if I had just been born. When I wake
I am breathing out of all proportion to myself.
My whole body is a lung; I am floating

above a doorway or a grave. And I know
I am in this breathing room as one
who understands how breath is passed
from father to son and passed back again.

At night, when my father comes to talk,
I tell him we have shared this body long enough.
He nods, like the speaker in a dream.
He knows that I know we're only talking.

Once there was a machine for breathing.
It would embrace the body and make a kind of love.
And when it was finished it would rise
like nothing at all above the earth

to drift through the daylight silence.
But at dark, in deep summer, if you thought you heard
something like your mother's voice calling you home,
you could lie down where you were and listen to the dead.

RAINBOW

                              Taking its time
through each of the seven vertebrae of light
the sun comes down. It is nineteen forty-nine.
You stand in the doorway drying your hands.
It is still summer, still raining.
The evening is everywhere gold: windows, grass,
the sun side of the trees. As if to speak
to someone you look back into the dark
of the house, call my name, go in. I know
I am dreaming again. Still, it is raining
and the sun shining . . . You come back out
into the doorway, shading your eyes. It looks
as if the whole sky is going down on one wing.
By now I have my hands above my eyes, listening.

WAGES

My Depression mother in a tin house.
My Depression father in a tin box.
It's raining. Nobody wants to get
out of bed, nobody wants the morning dark.

Her voice like money in a tin cup.
Her voice like money in a tin cup.
My father wept who would not work.

All over Ohio the mills are warming up
and whole grain in Kansas burning.
Nobody's starving, nobody's going to die.
We're sleeping till sunlight this morning.

But who will not work shall not eat.
Even my sleepwalking mother tells
this truth, cursing the cost of living.

DECEMBER, 1945

How the dry day goes, lapidary,
wind against the grain—

the gray grass, the kindling
of the whole stark tree,

the brick-and-straw burning of the sun,
field, fallow, flame:

my grandfather's foundry,
long into dark, cast iron, cast clay,

cast weed—stoke and bank, baked bread,
loaves the size of furnace doors,

lifted, left to cool all night, to make
of each day the requisite stones of hunger.

EARLY MEADOW-RUE

The fields in fog, the low, dull resonance of morning.

There never was an old country.
Only this privacy, the dream life of the deaf,
the girl looking into the mirror above her head,
prone in paralysis.

        And this one loneliness,
poverty or purity of choice, driving cold
in the general direction of the sun before dawn,
coffee in the truck, and bread, the cab light on,
and nobody, nobody else on the airstrip of the road,

going to work.

THE TREE

It looked like oak, white oak, oak of the oceans,
oak of the Lord, live oak, oak if a boy could choose.
The names, like ganglia, were the leaves, flesh

of our fathers. So Sundays I would stand
on a chair and trace, as on a county map,
back to the beginnings of cousins,

nomenclature. This branch, this root . . .
I could feel the weight of my body take hold,
toe in. I could see the same shape in my hand.

And if from the floor it looked like a cauliflower,
dried, dusted, pieced back together, paper—
my bad eyes awed by the detailed dead and named—

it was the stalk of the spine as it culminates at the brain,
a drawing I had seen in a book about the body, each leaf
inlaid until the man's whole back, root and stem, was veins.

RUTH

My grandmother and I planted marigolds. She did.
I watched. I was six, my hands jaundiced
    with the rubbings
of dandelions, sow-thistle, goat's-beard. She thought

I was dangerous with anything smaller than I was,
though she let me pick cherries, pull onions,
    put the bean
jars on the top pantry shelf. My hands wore the color

of work almost as well as yellow. I plowed the worms
for their copper. I pulled her flowers because
    they were gold
in the ground. I put them back now, just as I found

them. She is dead and part of the chemical compound
the grass is. These famous hands of mine are fouled.

1889–1976

ANOTHERING

The day my youngest sister is born
        it snows three inches
in April in Ohio. My mother says
        it's a cold sign:
cold sign, inside she's a weeper,
        repeats my sad father.

And true, for days she carries
        a weight, like water,
around inside her, as she carried
        that other, my sister,
for months. In there, she says,
        where it's empty.

BROTHERS & SISTERS

1

Even among your family you stand off to one side,
your big, dead face at last benign. The picture's
not dated, but everybody's poormouthed, pale, sun-
in-the-eye, the background data circa nineteen
sixty-nine. The photography is functional.
Your sisters look like part of the class, your
brothers part of the company. With some formality
each of you holds your own other hand. You're
practically the parent here, though it's Paul
who's about to complain to the camera: the angle's wrong,
too much sun. Everybody's blue or brown suit is shining.

2

We're out of the movies. The pictures don't lie,
Vivien Leigh is snow white Blanche DuBois. She has
a sister, the one everybody says you look like.
It is nineteen fifty-one, summer, and out on the sidewalk
the mere sun is blinding, tag-end. This is the matinee.

I saw you naked once, the lady at her bath. It's true,

you looked like somebody else. I had never seen so much
flesh. I ran the movie over and over. Pictures don't lie.
In the fifties photograph you still look like somebody's
brilliant sister, the girl in time, all face, too beautiful
but good, who's doting too completely on the boy.

3

In school we were told to draw our parents. Everybody
made moons—great pumpkin smiling moons, vegetable moons,
elliptical moons, moons like sad maps, eyes, ears, nose,
and chinless moons. We even cut black paper for cameos.
All of the faces floated in the dead air of pictures.

For years now their faces have run together. My father's
lives in my mother's as if by blood. Brother and sister.
She looks down at me from the dream as through a mirror.
She has the face of a child, somebody small, lunar.
Somebody's always standing by the bed. Sleep is the story

in which the child falls to the dead, rises, and is loved.

II

II

ANOTHERING

Mete unto wombe, and wombe eek unto mete

1

The room would be the inside of a greenhouse,
some desks in shadow, some in light,
the blackboard patched, stitches of chalk . . .
It would be late May, two weeks to go,
the sun like honey in our heads.

And we would have watched every day for months,
Alma sitting or Alma standing up.
We would have learned somewhere that fucking was
pumping and you could always tell
if a girl had by the size of her stomach.

2

Mary in light, Mary in shadow.
The angel lay down on one side,
the ghost on the other. Into
each ear saying: Child, be with
child, your father is with you.
And the angel kissed her mouth,
saying take this breath. And
the ghost entered her, saying
take this body. And she rose
filled with flesh, a woman.

3

Children with child. The night Alma
Schultz hanged herself her baby had
not been born. But it lived, blue ash,
blue coal. It came out into the room of
fathers twice tied to its past and flesh

of the flesh of her father. Alma was older
and taller. We were children. It was summer.
The dead go down and down, we were told,
in new clothes and a book. And rise among angels
and our father's ghost. In shadow, yes, in light.

SAY SUMMER/FOR MY MOTHER

I could give it back to you, perhaps in a season,
say summer. I could give you leaf back, green
grass, sky full of rain, root
that won't dig deeper, the names called out
just before sundown: *Linda back, Susy back,
Carolyn.* I could give you back supper
on the porch or the room without a breath
of fresh air, back the little tears in the heat,
the hot sleep on the kitchen floor,
back the talk in the great dark,
the voices low on the lawn
so the children can't hear,
say summer, say father, say mother:
Ruth and *Mary* and *Esther*, names in a book,
names I remember—I could give you back this name,
and back the breath to say it with—
we all know we'll die of our children—
back the tree bent over the water,
back the sun burning down,
back the witness back each morning.

PEPPERGRASS

Nothing you could know, or name, or say
in your sleep, nothing you'd remember,
poor-man's-pepper, wildflower, weed—
what the guidebook calls *the side
of the road*—as from the moon the earth
looks beautifully anonymous, this field
pennycress, this shepherd's purse, nothing
you could see: summer nights we'd look up
at the absolute dark, the stars, and turn like toys . . .

Nothing you could hold on to
but the wet grass, cold as morning.

We were windmills where the wind came from,
nothing, nothing you could name,
blowing the lights out, one by one.

LINOLEUM: BREAKING DOWN

Poor is cold feet in the morning, cold floor.
She would come out of her bedroom
with nothing on and say that her arm
was sore or that her leg was numb
or that her heart hurt her so much
she would have to lie down on the floor
right there and go to sleep. Go cold.
And we would lie down with her, my sister
and I, and she would tell us not to worry,
that it was all right, this is what happens,
like a bruise above the breast, we would
understand in time, body rich, body
poor, nothing is sure, nothing. And

outside it is just about to snow, and

I am up, sitting on the edge of the bed,
my feet almost flat on the floor, cold
as two coins dropped on marble. My mother
is dressed now, I am called out to see her
in her captain's chair. She has nothing
to say. She looks at me as if she were
looking at something. I feel I am standing
on her grave. Winter is one long morning.
She will get into the car, it will be
snowing, the car will go from here
to there, in time, the car's tracks,
like the scuff marks on linoleum,
will outlast a little traffic, then disappear.

GHAZAL/INSOMNIA

We lived in a block house. Day-lily, night-lily,
one window looking out, one window in.

Your voice tapped hollow every seam, each soft spot,
rang three bells in the three-hour-old morning.

And days closed down by rain, you almost sang.
That voice is hardly bearable that breaks—

the fox-orange of the flower in a slur of green.
Mother, that was hundreds of years ago,

in the century of pain. The lilies neither spin,
nor toil. Tomorrow, five bells at least, or none.

We lived in a block house. It is five a.m.
I'm here, you're here with first light, coffee, and the rain.

FOR ESTHER

From the back it looks like a porch,
portable, the filigree railing French.

And Truman, Bess and the girl each come out
waving, in short sleeves, because the heat
is worse than Washington.

The day is twelve hours old, Truman is talking.
You tell me to pay attention,

                              so I have my ball-
cap in my hands when he gets to the part that the sun

is suicidal, his dry voice barely audible above the train.

It makes a noise like steam.
He says, he says, he says.

His glasses silver in the sun. He says
there is never enough, and leans down to us.

2

Shultz and I put pennies on the track to make
the train jump. It jumps.

Afternoons you nap—one long pull of the body
through the heat.

                I go down to the depot
against orders; it's practically abandoned
except for the guy who hangs out

the mail and looks for pennies. He's president

of this place, he says. We pepper his B & O
brick building with tar balls when he's gone.

You hate the heat and sleep and let
your full voice go when I get caught.

You can't stand my noise or silence.
And I can hear a train in each bent coin.

You're thirty. I still seem to burden that young body.

3

Light bar, dark bar, all the way down. The trick is
if a train comes there is room for only the river.

I look down between the crossties at the Great Miami.
Three miles back, near home,

Kessler has already climbed to his station.
The trick is waiting for the whistle.

                                    I remember
your dream about bridges: how, as a child, they shook
you off, something the wind compelled.

You woke up holding on. And now this August morning

I don't know enough to be afraid or care.
I do my thinking here,

looking down at the long ladder on the water,
forty feet below.

4

The engine at idle, coasting in the yard, the call bell
back and forth, back and forth above the lull . . .

I hang on like the mail as the cars lock in
to one another, couple, and make a train.

The time I break my arm you swear
me to the ground—no more rivers,
no more side-car rides—

                     and stay up half
the night to rub my legs to sleep.

Sometimes you talk as if Roosevelt

were still alive. Recovery is memory.
I never broke my arm.

                  Back and forth. The names
of the states pass every day in front of us, single-file.

5

If a house were straw there'd be a wind,
if a house were wood there'd be a fire,

if a house were brick there'd be a track
and a train to tell the time.

                            I wish each passage
well—wind, fire, time, people on a train.
From here to there, three minutes, whistle-stop.

And the speech each night, the seconds clicking off.

The whole house shakes—or seems to. At intervals,
the ghost smoke fills

all the windows on the close-in side.
It's our weather. It's what we hear all night,
between Troy and anywhere, what you meant

to tell me, out of the body, out of the body travel.

THIS POEM

It is familiar language, like the lifetime leitmotif
of a vowel, the one pure sound you will ever make,

what you say to yourself in the little litany
of breathing.

But nothing like *the bicycle lay out
all night on the lawn.* The first voice I ever heard
I still hear, like the small talk in a daydream.

Przewalski's horse on the wall at Lascaux is language,
as in a child's drawing the voiceprint is simply visual,
what the eye overheard. Every voice we imagine will

eventually take form, as those we remember are
written down.

Here and here and here.

SMALL DARK STREETS

You are like
the woman in the doorway
who used to call
my name in the summer,
in the evening, over
and over, across the yards,
the woman in the window,
one light on,
supper, and the table set
since six,
the woman calling me home—

up and down, up
and down the stairs,
the woman who loved
clean floors and rain
on the streets after dark—

who knelt at my ear,
night after night,
whose story
could break your heart
if you listened, the woman
with her forehead pinned
to the wall,
the woman
who passed my small hand
over the dark part
of her body for luck.

WRONG SIDE OF THE RIVER

I watched you on the wrong side
of the river, waving. You were trying
to tell me something. You used both hands
and sort of ran back and forth,
as if to say *look behind you, look out
behind you.* I wanted to wave back.
But you began shouting and I didn't
want you to think I understood.
So I did nothing but stand still,
thinking that's what to do on the wrong side
of the river. After a while you did too.
We stood like that for a long time. Then
I raised a hand, as if to be called on,
and you raised a hand, as if to the same question.

SONNET

He says it's all one big bed anyway,
the whole fucking world. Sooner or later
all the lines of communication cross.
The girl wanders back and forth between
rooms. What does it matter? The body's
sweetbread: *the open grave of the soul.*
I lie down in yours with others. Freud says
every fuck is a foursome. I love
you. But the bodies are piling up.
And the girl wanders back and forth
between rooms. There's a dead planet out
there for each of us. That's why we fill
the earth with rooms and lie down together.
That's why I lie down in you with others.

LOVE POEM

And once, when I rose
from your body, it was like
water I had looked

into, water I had held.

FOR HOPE

I gave my word. And broke it. I gave
it again, broke it again, gave it a third time,
and broke it. So much for honor among wives.

There is a woman you love, in whose face
shines your own. Heart, you say to her,
I give you gold instead. Word, that great

weight, tied like a leper's shadow to everything,
I give back to the dark, to nothing, where
it came from, the place under the tongue.

I give it back and then I give it back again,
because *man who is born of woman* and *word
made flesh, one flesh*—these too are broken.

This woman you love, in whose face shines
your own, like an oath of sun—Heart,
you say to her, my word, silence is golden.

OUT-OF-THE-BODY TRAVEL

I

And then he would lift this finest
of furniture to his big left shoulder
and tuck it in and draw the bow
so carefully as to make the music

almost visible on the air. And play
and play until a whole roomful of the sad
relatives mourned. They knew this was
drawing of blood, threading and rethreading

the needle. They saw even in my father's
face how well he understood the pain
he put them to—his raw, red cheek
pressed against the cheek of the wood . . .

2

And in one stroke he brings the hammer
down, like mercy, so that the young bull's
legs suddenly fly out from under it . . .
While in the dream he is the good angel

in Chagall, the great ghost of his body
like light over the town. The violin
sustains him. It is pain remembered.
Either way, I know if I wake up cold,

and go out into the clear spring night,
still dark and precise with stars,
I will feel the wind coming down hard
like his hand, in fever, on my forehead.

SUCH COUNSELS

My father would always come
back from the barn
as if he had been in conference.
He had farm in him the way
some men have pain.
Every night the feed, the one
thing to get him home straight.

Still, he was a one-armed man,
toting his bottle
like a book of hours.
And he could sleep standing.
Each year to kill those cattle
he had to drink a week in a day
to stay cold sober.

HORSE IN THE CAGE

Its face, as long as an arm, looks down & down.

Then the iron gate sound of the cage swings shut
above the bed, a bell as big as the room: quarter-
moon of the head, its nose, its whole lean body
pressed against its cell . . .

I watched my father hit a horse in the face once.

It had come down to feed across the fence.
My father, this stranger, wanted to ride.
Perhaps he wanted only to talk. Anyway,
he hit the ground and something broke.

As a child I never understood how an animal
could sleep standing. In my dream the horse
rocks in a cage too small, so the cage swings.

I still wake up dreaming, in front of a long face.
That day I hugged the ground hard.

Who knows if my heartbroken father was meant
to last longer than his last good drunk.
They say it's like being kicked by a horse.

You go down, your knees hug up.
You go suddenly wide awake, and the gate shuts.

HAYDENVILLE BLOCK

He could be checking the walls out
now, level and square,
the quality of surfaces,
as in a mirror, for flaws,

as in a story, the house
your father built was flawed,
half-finished, the twin
ribs of the roof honed

hollow by the wind . . .
Or he could, if he wanted,
lay down his tools
and lie down with them,

as in every history
of the fathers who build
from the ground up—
firebrick, waterbrick, man-

made stone. But nothing gets done.
Like poverty, the story
is round. He traveled
a hundred miles to Haydenville

for the blocks to build
his house. They were tile,
the color of the earth. Even
Haydenville, one block long, is pure

terra cotta, people on porches.
The story is round.
He started laying brick that night.
He made, in his mind, a tower.

There was snow in the air,
the wickerwork of the moon.
By winter he was building fires
to warm the early dark.

TWO POEMS

I

Sometimes sixteen hours a day,
back-breaking, belly-aching hours,
dark at both ends, and at night
the two of us sparring in the kitchen,
you, blind drunk, shouting the walls down
I'm a dead tree in this room
Mornings you wept.

You sat on the edge of the bed,
you knew you were dying.
It was always five o'clock in the dark.
Your body was falling, even the heart
had to float. The blood signs were
everywhere. You were a man rising
to go to work.

When shall we be done growing?
Melville asks. Jackstraw hammered
into the wood. All day, in labor,
the wind was blowing: how many times
I thought I saw land. And if he is dead
and the door closed, don't knock.
Bury at sea.

2

There can be no labor
like theirs, no pain,
no thought, no word, as passed
from dumb mouth to deaf ear,
no wish, no dream in no sleep.
A nation of silence, a night nation,
a nation in which stone is the source of light.
The nation of the dead numbers
one hundred times one hundred million.
And more, much more. Whitman,
looking down from the web
of the great stars, saw this compost,
this earth turning "harmless
and stainless on its axis."
What he could not see was the mill-wheel
in hell that makes it work. The day
turning into the dark turning into the day.
In one dream I see my back-breaking father
at the wheel. He is grinding bone
back into dust. He looks like a miller
covered with flour. He works
his shift only to lie down
among the million
upon million
and rise again,
individual, to the wheel.

NOW THAT MY FATHER LIES DOWN
BESIDE ME

We lie in that other darkness, ourselves.
There is less than the width of my left hand
between us. I can barely breathe,
but the light breathes easily,
wind on water across our two still bodies.

I cannot even turn to see him.
I would not touch him. Nor would I lift
my arm into the crescent of a moon.
(There is no star in the sky of this room,
only the light fashioning fish along the walls.
They swim and swallow one another.)

I dream we lie under water,
caught in our own sure drift.
A window, white shadow, trembles over us.
Light breaks into a moving circle.
He would not speak and I would not touch him.

It is an ocean under here.
Whatever two we were, we become
one falling body, one breath. Night lies down
at the sleeping center—no fish, no shadow,
no single, turning light. And I would not touch him
who lies deeper in the drifting dark than life.

AFTER GRIEF

When you woke among them,
when you rose,
when you got up and they asked you
what you were—is it named?—
and you in your new clothes
and face and body lined dry with newspaper,

when you climbed out of the coffin
and began to walk,
alive (*like a rainbow* one of them said),
without a word, in this place of skull and femur,
stone and the sounds of water, when you walked up
to the one talking, his face a face
of the moon, and started to speak, he said

no need, I know who you are.

All this recorded in the first book, The Dream,
in the blessing of the death
of each day.

And tonight, bedded down,
the mind adrift, the body just a few feet
from the earth, it is written

there is the river,
go wash yourself.
And you asked

what is this place? And the one
without a face answered
look around you, this is where you are.

I remember how even near the end
you would go out to your garden
just before dark, in the blue air,
and brood over the failures
of corn or cabbage
or the crooked row
but meaning the day had once more
failed for you.

I watched you as any son watches his father,
like prophecy.

And in my mind I counted the thousand
things to say.

And tonight, again, it is written
that the one talking said
Father, forgive everything.
leave these clothes, this body.
lie down in the water.
be whole.

And having done so, you rose

among them, who are called The Bones,
without flesh or face.

All this recorded in the dream unending.

The first death was the death of the father.
And whosoever be reborn in sons
so shall they be also reborn.

In the Book of the Dead are names
the weight of the continents.
At each rising of the waters
shall the earth be washed.

This is the dream that holds the planet
in place.

And you, my anonymous father,
be with me when I wake.

STANLEY PLUMLY was born in Barnesville, Ohio, and grew up in the lumber and farming regions of Virginia and Ohio. He has taught at several universities, most recently at the Writers' Workshop at the University of Iowa and at Princeton University. His *In the Outer Dark* won the Delmore Schwartz Memorial Award, and he held a Guggenheim Fellowship in poetry for 1973–1974.